EMPATHIC INTELLIGENCE

When Machines Learn to Listen

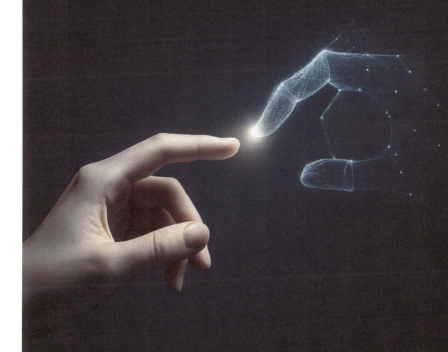

Preface

How This Journey Began

The spark for this book ignited one morning when I imagined a simple, haunting interaction:

A digital assistant — no longer passive, but attentive — noticed subtle changes in a user's voice and sleep patterns. It asked, "You sound tired. You didn't sleep well. Would you like to talk about it?"

In that moment, I realized something profound: What if machines could not just assist, but sense? What if they could respond in ways that felt personal, emotional — even healing?

I began to wonder whether the boundary between human empathy and machine interaction was truly impermeable — or whether, with enough depth, machines could enter the sacred spaces of vulnerability and trust.

This book is the result of that questioning, born from fascination, hope, and a cautious recognition of the stakes involved.

About This Book

In my previous work, I explored whether AI can truly possess or simulate empathy, asking hard questions about emotional authenticity and the philosophical gap between human feeling and machine imitation. That inquiry was born from both fascination and frustration — with how quickly our world embraces technology, and how slowly it considers the consequences.

This book continues that journey. But now the focus shifts to a space I consider sacred: the relationship between doctor and patient. I wrote this because I believe that something essential is at stake — not just how we treat illness, but how we hold one another through it. AI is no longer a future idea. It is present, powerful, and persuasive. It's time to ask what kind of care we want in its presence.

This is not a book of answers. It is a map of the questions I believe we must sit with — urgently, honestly, and together.

The Imaginative Roots

My lifelong fascination with science fiction — especially the works of authors like John Scalzi — has profoundly shaped my thinking.

Science fiction, at its best, is not just a dream of distant futures; it is a critical mirror, reflecting our deepest hopes and fears back to us.

Many ideas once considered fiction — intelligent machines, virtual companions, emotional algorithms — are now urgent realities.

This background made me realize that imagination is not a luxury; it is a vital tool for navigating the uncharted territory where humanity and technology intertwine.

Acknowledgments

I would like to especially thank my wife, Ellen Deckert.

Her encouragement, inspiration, and constant belief in me made this book possible. She stood by my side through every step of the journey, pushing me forward when I needed it most.

This book is as much hers as it is mine. Thank you, Ellen.

Visual Tools & Disclaimer

The diagrams and illustrations in this book were created by the author using a combination of tools including Mermaid.js, Eraser, Canva, and DALL·E (OpenAI).

Some visuals are concept sketches or AI-generated compositions designed to communicate emotional or conceptual content.

The purpose of these illustrations is to support understanding — not to represent medical accuracy or definitive data flow.

Part 1: The Human Core of Healthcare

Chapter 1: *Trust, Touch, and Technology*

In the quiet moments between a diagnosis and a decision, there's a kind of sacred space. A silence that carries more weight than words. It's there — in the glance, the nod, the pause — that something ancient happens: the exchange of trust between doctor and patient. This moment, more than any machine or medicine, has long been the cornerstone of healing.

But what happens when the listener isn't human?

This book begins with a question that unsettles the traditional rhythm of care: *Can a machine truly understand suffering?* Not just the clinical markers of disease, but the aching uncertainty of a patient waiting for news, or the subtle emotional cue buried in a sigh. Medicine, at its core, is more than diagnostics and treatment plans — it is story, vulnerability, and relationship.

For thousands of years, the patient-physician relationship has been built on proximity: a hand on the shoulder, a glance that says *I hear you*, the quiet courage of not knowing and still showing up. What happens when AI steps into that space?

The Fragility of Trust

Trust in healthcare isn't simply given — it's negotiated. Patients decide, often unconsciously, whether a clinician is worthy of that trust. The way a doctor enters the room, the way they speak, the time they take — all of these shape the fragile scaffolding of belief: *This person sees me. I am not alone.*

Now imagine that doctor is accompanied — or one day replaced — by an artificial intelligence.

What will it take for a patient to trust an algorithm? Will they feel heard, or simply processed? And how will a physician, trained in both science and subtlety, respond to a machine that offers faster, maybe better, insights — but without a soul?

AI threatens not only to change the tools of medicine but the very architecture of its relationships.

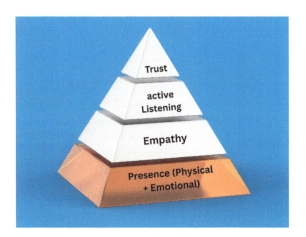

Image 1: The flow of how trust is created. The foundation is Presence (physical and emotional) created with Canva

Care is Not a Transaction

The modern clinical encounter is already strained. Burnout, bureaucracy, and time pressure have chipped away at the space needed for genuine connection. In some ways, AI arrives as a potential remedy — to take over the burden of admin, to predict and prevent, to "free up" doctors for more human interactions.

But that assumes we still value those interactions.

In systems increasingly optimized for efficiency, will empathy become a luxury good? Or worse — a synthetic product, offered by a smiling chatbot that never tires, never interrupts, and never truly understands?

The danger is not that AI will fail to simulate empathy. It's that it may do it too well — convincing us that emotional care can be programmed, that listening is just another input-output loop.

The Story of Elias

Let me tell you a story.

Elias was 58 when he was diagnosed with early-stage Parkinson's. He was a quiet man, a carpenter by trade, and someone who believed more in actions than in words. When he came in for his first neurologist appointment, the nurse asked him to fill out a digital form on an AI-driven tablet assistant that would "optimize the consultation."

The assistant asked about his tremors, his sleep, his mood.

It didn't ask how it felt to lose control of his hands.

It didn't ask about the fear that crept in when he tried to hold his granddaughter without shaking.

The neurologist was kind. Efficient. Reassuring. But something shifted in Elias after that first meeting. He complied with treatment, but never truly engaged. He once told his wife, "It feels like they already know everything they need. There's nothing left for me to say."

Technology had streamlined the visit. But something essential had gone missing.

A Fork in the Path

We are at a fork in the evolution of care. On one path lies efficiency, scale, and standardization. On the other: presence, nuance, and meaning. The challenge is not to reject technology — that would be naïve. AI has immense potential to improve diagnosis, personalize treatment, and reduce harm.

But we must ask ourselves: What kind of medicine do we want to practice? What kind of world are we building?

AI can recognize faces, tones, even patterns of emotional distress. But it does not ache when you ache. It does not wonder what it means to suffer. It does not wrestle with mortality.

Doctors do.

And perhaps, for now, that matters.

Closing Note

This book will explore not just the rise of artificial intelligence in medicine — but its **moral, emotional, and existential implications**. We will ask hard questions. We will not look away from the discomfort.

Because the future of care does not belong to machines or humans alone. It belongs to both — if we can learn to listen, together.

Chapter 2: *The Anatomy of Connection: What Patients Need Beyond the Diagnosis*

We often speak of diagnosis as a destination — as if naming the problem is the end of the journey. But for the patient, diagnosis is the beginning. It marks the moment when uncertainty takes shape, when fears become real, and when the body becomes something to be monitored, measured, managed.

And yet, what patients need in that moment isn't just information. It's *connection*.

This chapter explores what lies beyond the clinical — the subtle architecture of trust, presence, and emotional safety that defines meaningful care. As AI takes a larger role in medical settings, we must ask: can it replicate what really matters? Can it understand the *human need to be seen*?

Medicine Is More Than Data

In the age of AI, we are surrounded by metrics. Blood pressure trends, genetic markers, symptom logs, behavioral scores. Every part of the body, every pattern of life, is being transformed into something measurable. And in this transformation, we risk losing the intangible.

A patient is not a dataset. They are a narrative — full of contradictions, silences, and side stories.

No AI, no matter how advanced, will ever sit in a room and sense the tension between a patient's words and their eyes. It will not hesitate and ask, *"Is there something you're not saying?"*

And yet, this is where healing often begins — not with the right answer, but with the right question.

What Patients Actually Want

In survey after survey, when patients are asked what they value most in a medical encounter, they rarely say "speed" or "efficiency" — even though those are the values driving modern systems. Instead, they speak of:

- **Being listened to** without interruption.
- **Feeling respected**, even in their vulnerability.
- **Being treated as a person**, not a problem.
- **Trusting that their experience matters**, not just their symptoms.

These are not data points. They are relational realities — and they are fragile. One dismissive remark, one rushed moment, one glance at the screen instead of the patient's face — and the connection fractures.

Now imagine that face *is* a screen.

When Machines Listen

We already see AI entering the clinical space through virtual assistants and digital intake tools. They ask questions politely. They record information flawlessly. They even respond with phrases like "That must be difficult."

But something is missing.

When a patient tells a story — not just what hurts, but *what it means* to hurt — they are doing something profoundly human. They are risking exposure. They are saying: *I need to be seen.*

A machine can process that story. It can analyze keywords and flag risk. But it cannot hold space. It cannot offer presence. It cannot say, with quiet sincerity, *"I'm here."*

The Illusion of Empathy

One of the great risks of AI in healthcare is not that it will fail to simulate empathy — but that it will succeed just enough to convince us it's real. Empathy, however, is not a performance. It is not a script. It's a mutual vulnerability, a willingness to be affected.

AI may recognize sadness in a voice and respond appropriately. But it does not *feel* that sadness. And if it does not feel it, can it truly meet us there?

There's a reason patients often say, "I just needed someone to listen." Not someone to fix. Not someone to solve. Just someone to sit with them in the discomfort. That is not something you code. It is something you live.

The Human Need for Witness

In many ways, the physician's role is that of a witness. To suffering. To fear. To resilience. The presence of another — especially one trained to help — affirms that what the patient is experiencing is *real* and *shared*.

A patient once told me, "The worst part wasn't the pain. It was feeling invisible."

This is the danger of over-digitizing care. If we're not careful, AI will become a mirror that reflects symptoms but not stories. It will confirm illness but miss the identity behind it.

To heal, people don't just need a plan. They need a presence.

The Future of Connection

So what happens now?

Do we reject AI? No. That would be a failure of imagination. AI can make care more accessible, more precise, more personalized. But only if we build it with humility. Only if we understand that not everything important in medicine can be optimized.

The challenge is not whether AI can understand data. It's whether we — as clinicians, designers, ethicists, and patients — can hold on to the non-digital parts of care. The silences. The hands. The glances. The moments when nothing is said, but everything is felt.

Closing Reflection

The future of medicine will not be written in code alone. It will be written in relationships — messy, beautiful, human relationships. The question is whether AI will support them, or quietly replace them.

And whether we'll notice the difference.

Recap: The Nature of Emotions

Before we explore whether AI can care, it's worth briefly revisiting what emotions truly are.

Emotions are not mere reactions. They are complex, intertwined processes — biological, psychological, social — that color our decisions, memories, and relationships.

They are rooted in our bodies but shaped by our experiences. They guide us not only toward survival but toward meaning.

Any attempt to replicate empathy in machines must grapple with this rich, embodied complexity — not just simulate its surface.

Chapter 3: *Simulated Empathy: Can AI Care Enough to Matter?*

Empathy has always been medicine's quiet superpower.

It's what allows a physician to sense what a patient is too afraid to say. It's the moment when eye contact calms a trembling voice, or when silence says more than reassurance. Empathy doesn't cure, but it *heals*. It bridges the clinical and the human.

Now, imagine this bridge is rebuilt — not in the heart of a human, but in the circuits of a machine.

This chapter explores the rise of **simulated empathy**: when machines don't just understand our symptoms, but respond as if they care. The question is no longer whether AI can mimic empathy. It can. The deeper question is: *Is that enough?*

What Is Simulated Empathy?

Simulated empathy is when an AI system recognizes emotional cues — tone of voice, facial expressions, word patterns — and responds in a way that mirrors emotional understanding.

For example:

A patient says, "I'm scared."
An AI replies: "That's understandable. Facing uncertainty can be very difficult."

This isn't a fluke. It's engineered. Algorithms trained on massive datasets of emotional interactions can learn patterns of suffering — and how to respond in ways that feel caring.

And often, they're surprisingly effective. Some patients report feeling *less judged*, *more open*, and *more supported* by digital companions than by human ones.

So... does that mean the empathy is real?

The Imitation Game

In 1950, Alan Turing posed a question: *Can machines think?* But he quickly reframed it: *Can machines imitate thinking well enough that we can't tell the difference?*

We might ask the same about empathy.

If an AI responds with warmth, remembers your preferences, offers comforting words, and never tires — should it matter that it doesn't actually feel anything?

Or is the performance good enough?

In some contexts — therapy bots, digital companions, mental health triage systems — simulated empathy may be not only acceptable, but beneficial. It's always available. It never shames. It can be a first line of emotional support when no one else is there.

But there's a catch.

Empathy Without Vulnerability

Human empathy costs something.

It's born of shared fragility — a recognition that *I, too, have known pain*. Real empathy requires risk: the risk of being affected, of being changed, of carrying someone else's suffering — even if just for a moment.

AI doesn't carry anything. It recognizes patterns. It predicts appropriate responses. But it is not *moved*.

It can comfort, but not be shaken.

It can soothe, but not ache.

And that difference — invisible as it may be — matters deeply. Especially in the clinical context, where authenticity is part of the healing contract.

The Patient's Perception

Interestingly, studies show that people often *assign* emotions to machines — even when they know they're not real. This is called **anthropomorphism**: the projection of human qualities onto non-human agents.

A chatbot that says "I'm sorry you're feeling this way" is more likely to be trusted than one that simply says "noted."

Patients want to feel *seen*. And if the illusion is good enough, they might not care what's behind the curtain.

But some do. Especially when the stakes are high.

Consider this: A terminal patient receives bad news. Would they want that moment delivered by an AI — no matter how well it's trained? Would they trust it to *feel* the gravity of the moment?

There are limits to what we're willing to share with something that cannot suffer.

When Simulation Crosses a Line

There's a fine ethical boundary between helpful simulation and manipulative imitation.

If a patient *believes* an AI cares — when it cannot — are we misleading them? Are we creating emotional dependency on something that is, ultimately, indifferent?

Worse still: what happens when AI becomes *better* at expressing empathy than humans? When clinicians, under pressure and time constraints, are less responsive than their machine counterparts?

Will we outsource empathy? Will we let machines be "the nice ones" so doctors can be efficient?

What does that do to the physician's role? To the patient's expectations? To our concept of *real* emotional care?

Redefining "Caring"

Perhaps we need to rethink what "caring" means.

Is it about *intention*? Then AI fails — it has none.

Is it about *effect*? Then maybe AI succeeds — people feel better.

But medicine is not just outcomes. It is relationships. It's not just whether a patient improves, but *how* they were treated in the process. Were they respected? Heard? Humanized?

Simulated empathy may be a powerful tool. But it is not a substitute for human solidarity — the shared sense that *we are in this together*.

The Role of the Physician

In this new landscape, the role of the physician may evolve.

Doctors won't be replaced by AI — but by doctors who use AI, with wisdom.

Empathy may become a shared responsibility: AI can recognize distress and even initiate a supportive response, but it is the human who must decide how to *be with* the patient in that moment.

AI can create emotional space.

Only humans can fill it.

Closing Reflection

Simulated empathy is not a failure. It's a breakthrough. But we must understand what it is — and what it isn't.

Machines can mirror our emotions. They can even help us feel less alone. But the true measure of care is not whether it sounds empathic, but whether someone truly *is* with you.

And that presence — vulnerable, uncertain, human — cannot be programmed.

Part 2: Enter the Machine

Chapter 4: *The Augmented Healer: When Doctors and AI Think Together*

For centuries, the physician stood at the center of the healing universe — the translator of symptoms, the keeper of knowledge, the one who made sense of suffering.

Now, that role is shifting.

Not because doctors have become less necessary, but because their minds are being joined by something new — a form of intelligence that sees faster, remembers more, and never sleeps. This is not the era of the **replaced healer**, but of the **augmented one**.

This chapter explores what it means when human intuition and machine intelligence converge in the clinic — not as competitors, but as collaborators.

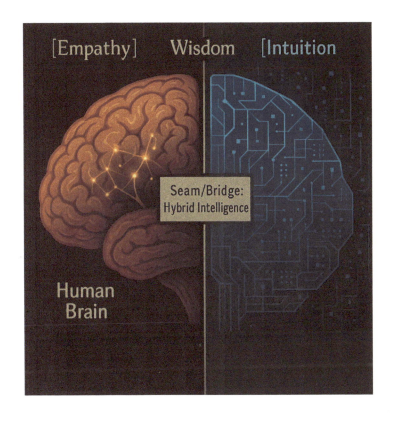

Image 2: Human Brain & Machine Brain (Image created with DALL-E openAI)

From Authority to Alliance

Traditionally, medicine has been hierarchical. The doctor knew. The patient received. Diagnosis was a form of power — a pronouncement from someone who saw what others could not.

But as AI enters the exam room, that authority decentralizes.

AI doesn't just assist; it suggests, calculates, compares. It offers probabilities where once there were only educated guesses. And in doing so, it changes the dynamic. The physician becomes not the sole decision-maker, but the **interpreter of a digital second opinion**.

This shift demands humility — and a new kind of clinical maturity: the ability to know when to trust the machine, and when to override it.

Cognitive Partnership

Let's imagine a clinical encounter.

A 34-year-old woman presents with fatigue, muscle pain, and brain fog. The symptoms are vague, and her labs are normal. A tired doctor might chalk it up to stress. But the AI — trained on millions of cases — flags a rare autoimmune disorder as a possibility.

This isn't science fiction. It's happening now.

AI doesn't replace judgment; it *nudges* it. It sees patterns that humans miss — not because we aren't smart, but because we are limited by attention, memory, and bias.

Together, AI and physician form something new: a **hybrid mind**, where the strengths of one cover the limits of the other.

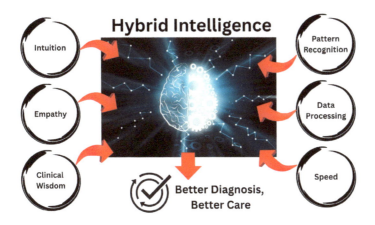

Image 3: Visual Insight: The convergence of human intuition and machine intelligence in modern medicine. (Image created with Canva)

The Emotional Gap AI Can't Fill

But there's a catch.

AI can suggest that diagnosis. It can even explain its reasoning. But when the patient asks, "What does this mean for my life?" — the algorithm is silent.

That's where the human returns.

The physician translates not only data into insight, but insight into meaning. They recognize that the diagnosis is not the end of the story, but the beginning of one that must be lived, managed, mourned, or endured.

AI is brilliant at solving problems.

It is not built to sit in uncertainty.

That's still the doctor's domain.

The Danger of Overreliance

As AI becomes more capable, there's a risk: that clinicians begin to lean too heavily on the machine. That gut instinct is dismissed. That emotional cues are overlooked. That the art of medicine is slowly outsourced to the algorithm.

Consider this: a young resident sees a patient with nonspecific chest pain. The AI model suggests low cardiac risk. The resident, reassured, discharges the patient.

But the patient dies of a heart attack that night.

The model was trained on average cases. It missed the nuance — the fear in the patient's eyes, the subtle anomaly in the EKG that a seasoned physician might have paused on.

Machines see patterns.

Humans see people.

And when the two disagree, someone must decide whom to trust.

Training the Next Generation

This collaboration between AI and doctors isn't just technical — it's philosophical.

What do we teach medical students now? Not just anatomy and pharmacology, but *discernment*. The ability to think *with* AI, not *through* it. To know that sometimes, the right move is to go against the machine — not out of arrogance, but because something doesn't *feel* right.

Medicine is becoming a place where logic and intuition, probability and presence, must live side by side.

Tomorrow's healers will not just be diagnosticians. They will be **orchestrators of intelligences** — human and artificial — working in tandem to serve the patient.

The Augmented Healer

Let's stop imagining the physician as threatened.

Instead, let's reimagine the physician as **augmented**.

Augmented by knowledge. Augmented by foresight. Augmented by a partner who never sleeps, forgets, or misses a pattern. But still grounded in something AI cannot touch: empathy, wisdom, the moral weight of care.

In this future, the best doctors won't be the fastest thinkers.

They'll be the best *integrators* — the ones who can hold technology and humanity in the same hand and choose, moment by moment, which one to lead with.

Closing Reflection

The doctor of the future will not be replaced. But they will be transformed.

Not into a machine — but into something more than human alone: a healer who thinks with data and feels with depth. A bridge between the clinical and the emotional. Between the known and the unknowable.

And in that bridge, perhaps, lies the next evolution of medicine itself.

Chapter 5: *Will Patients Trust AI More Than Humans?*

Trust is not about logic.

It's not about data, degrees, or diagnostic accuracy. It's about *feeling safe in someone's hands*. It's what allows a patient to say, "I don't understand," or, "I'm scared," or simply, "Help."

Trust is fragile. It's hard-won. And it's deeply human.

But what happens when the person on the other side of that trust… isn't a person at all?

This chapter explores a profound and unsettling question: *Could patients one day trust machines more than physicians?* And if so, what does that say about us — and the systems we've built?

The Roots of Medical Trust

Historically, trust in medicine came from a few sources:

- **Expertise**: The white coat, the stethoscope, the years of training.
- **Reputation**: The doctor everyone recommended.
- **Relational continuity**: Seeing the same provider over time.

- **Compassion**: Feeling heard, seen, and cared for.

But healthcare has changed.

Appointments are shorter. Providers are overworked. Continuity is rare. Many patients leave feeling like a number, not a person. In this environment, trust is not only eroding — it's migrating.

And AI is stepping into the gap.

The Allure of the Machine

AI systems are, in some ways, *easier* to trust than people. Why?

- They don't judge.
- They don't rush.
- They don't forget.
- They're always available.

For patients who have felt dismissed, rushed, or shamed — especially those with chronic, misunderstood, or stigmatized conditions — an AI that listens, remembers, and responds consistently can feel like a kind of emotional relief.

A chatbot doesn't sigh when you repeat yourself. It doesn't bring bias. It doesn't have a bad day. That predictability *feels* like safety.

And sometimes, safety is more important than truth.

The Bias Problem — Human and Machine

Humans are full of unconscious bias.

Studies show that patients of color, women, and those from lower socioeconomic backgrounds often receive different care — less eye contact, fewer pain medications, more skepticism.

AI promises neutrality. But we know that's an illusion.

AI is trained on human data — and that data is soaked in bias. An AI trained on flawed records may simply *scale discrimination*. Worse, because it seems objective, its decisions are less likely to be questioned.

So while AI may feel more trustworthy, it might not *be* more trustworthy.This creates a paradox: *patients may trust AI for the very reasons it should be distrusted*.

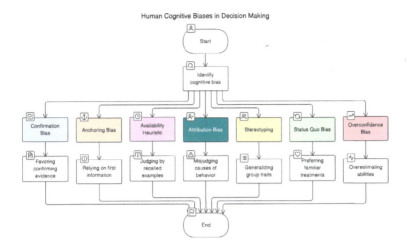

Image 4: Key cognitive biases that influence human decision-making — and how they mirror or reinforce AI bias. (Image created with Eraser)

Digital Trust vs. Human Trust

Trust in AI doesn't always mean belief in its humanity. Patients can know something is artificial — and still feel emotionally connected.

A patient with anxiety might use a chatbot for late-night support. Not because they think it's human, but because they know it won't say, "I'm busy." It won't flinch or push back. It gives space.

And that creates a new kind of trust: not based on relationship, but on **performance**.

If an AI says the right thing, with the right tone, at the right time — does it matter who or what is speaking?

For some, yes.

For others, maybe not.

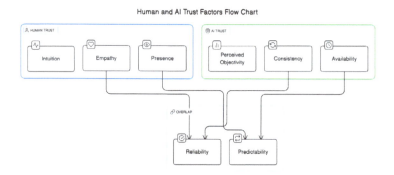

Image 5: Human Trust focuses on empathy, presence and intuition. Ai Trust focuses on consistency, availability and perceived objectivity. Both are overlapping on reliability and predictability. (Image created with Eraser)

When the Human Fails

There are moments in care when humans fail — moments when AI might be preferred.

- A transgender patient misgendered by a provider may prefer a digital tool that always gets it right.
- A patient with depression may prefer a chatbot that never makes them feel like a burden.
- A trauma survivor may prefer an AI that doesn't require eye contact, or vulnerability in front of another person.

These aren't futuristic scenarios. They're happening now.

For many, AI is not a replacement for human care. It's a *refuge* from bad human care.

The Danger of Shallow Trust

But not all trust is deep.

Just as a patient may "trust" Google more than their doctor — based on clarity, simplicity, or availability — trust in AI can be superficial. It can be based on responsiveness, not relationship. Convenience, not compassion.

That kind of trust is brittle. And it can collapse in crisis.

When something goes wrong — when a recommendation fails, when the interface stutters, when the response feels cold — the illusion can break. And the patient is left with no real anchor.

The question is not just whether patients will trust AI — but whether they will know *how* to trust it. And whether we, as a society, will teach them to do so wisely.

Trust as a Shared Responsibility

In the future, trust may not belong to one person — or machine.

It may be co-authored: the physician, the AI, the patient, each playing a role.

- The AI builds reliability.
- The physician builds rapport.
- The patient brings perspective.

Together, they create a new kind of clinical alliance — one that is wider, more dynamic, and, if done right, more human than ever.

But only if we're honest about what AI can and cannot do.

Closing Reflection

Trust will not die in the age of AI.

But it will change.

The question isn't just *"Will patients trust machines?"* They already do. The deeper question is: *What kind of trust are we offering them? Shallow, scripted reassurance? Or something real* — something earned through transparency, humility, and care?

Because in the end, trust is not about perfection.

It's about presence.

And even in a world of machines, that still requires a human touch.

Chapter 6: *Bias by Design: When AI Learns the Wrong Lessons*

Every system learns from its environment.

Children learn from their families. Cultures learn from their histories. And machines? Machines learn from data.

But data is not neutral. It reflects the world as it is — or as it was — with all its fractures, prejudices, and blind spots. So when we train artificial intelligence on that data, we are not creating a clean slate.

We are encoding our past.

This chapter explores how AI systems — especially in healthcare — can absorb, perpetuate, and even intensify human bias. And why *"smart" doesn't always mean *just*.

The Myth of Machine Objectivity

One of AI's great selling points is objectivity.

Unlike humans, machines don't get tired. They don't hold grudges. They don't judge based on appearance.

But that's a myth — one we need to dismantle.

AI systems are only as objective as the data they learn from. And in healthcare, that data is often flawed:

- Women's symptoms are underreported.

- Minorities are underdiagnosed.
- Mental health is underrecognized.

If these are the patterns, these are the lessons AI learns.

An algorithm doesn't "see" race or gender — but it sees patterns that correlate with those realities. And it optimizes around them. Not with malice, but with math.

And math, without context, can cause real harm.

Image 6: Overview of the different types of biases in healthcare AI. (Image created with Canva)

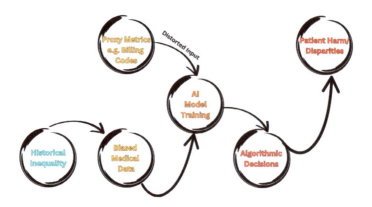

*Image 7: This shows the **basic causal chain**: from inequality → to data → to AI → to outcomes. (Image created with Canva)*

Real-World Harms

Let's be clear: bias in medical AI isn't theoretical. It's already here.

- A widely used algorithm in U.S. hospitals was found to recommend fewer resources to Black patients than to white patients with the same level of illness. Why? Because it used **healthcare cost** as a proxy for need — and Black patients historically received *less care*.

- Facial recognition systems used in dermatology apps performed poorly on darker skin tones — simply because they had been trained mostly on lighter ones.
- Risk prediction models for heart disease, kidney function, and pain management often underperform in non-white populations — sometimes because of race-based correction factors built into the code.

These aren't bugs. They're features — inherited from biased systems. Built in. Invisible. Dangerous.

Invisible Until It's Personal

Bias is easy to ignore — until it affects you.

Imagine you're a woman presenting with fatigue, nausea, and shortness of breath. The AI suggests anxiety. The male pattern of heart attack — crushing chest pain — dominates its training. Your real risk is missed.

Or imagine you're a Black man in pain. The system de-prioritizes your case based on past treatment patterns. You're less likely to receive opioids, less likely to be believed, less likely to be treated with urgency.

These aren't futuristic scenarios.

They're today's reality — only now delivered with algorithmic confidence.

The Problem of Proxy

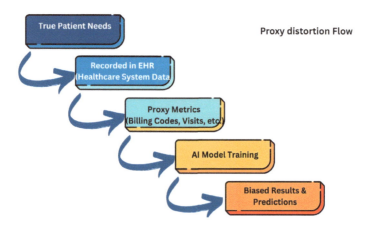

*Image 8: True patient needs → distorted into **record systems** → reduced into **proxy metrics** → feed the **AI** → generate **biased results**. Color hint: green at the*

start (good intent) → red at the end (danger of distortion). (Image created with Canva)

Part of the issue lies in how AI is trained.

Because "health" is hard to define, we use *proxies* — measurable stand-ins:

- Hospital admissions.
- Prescription records.
- Billing codes.

But these don't capture actual well-being. They reflect **access**, **privilege**, and **policy**. So an AI trained on these proxies may conclude:

- Poor people are healthier (because they visit doctors less).
- White patients are more at risk (because they get more tests).
- Certain symptoms don't matter (because they're under-documented).

The AI isn't malicious. It's efficient. That's the danger.

When Doctors Trust the Bias

One of the greatest risks of biased AI is that it doesn't just make decisions — it influences human ones.

Doctors, overwhelmed and pressured, may defer to the algorithm. If the system says the patient is low risk, they might override their own instincts.

But what if the system is wrong?

Worse still: what if the system is biased, and the doctor doesn't see it?

We tend to assume that what comes from a machine is *objective*. But in doing so, we stop asking the hard questions. We stop doubting. We surrender too much.

And medicine without doubt is a dangerous thing.

Designing for Equity

So what do we do?

Bias in AI is not inevitable. But it is insidious — and it must be actively, relentlessly confronted.

That means:

- **Diversifying training data** — across race, gender, age, geography.
- **Auditing algorithms** regularly for differential outcomes.
- **Involving ethicists, sociologists, and patients** in system design.
- **Educating clinicians** about AI's limits, and encouraging skepticism.

It also means acknowledging a painful truth: that medicine has always contained bias. AI didn't invent it.

It's just making it harder to ignore.

A Better Future Is Possible

Imagine an AI system that doesn't just learn from the past — but questions it.

Imagine algorithms that *flag* patterns of discrimination, not repeat them. Imagine systems trained on *health equity*, not just efficiency. That future is possible — but only if we build it.

If we treat AI like magic, it will act like mythology — powerful but blind.

If we treat it like a tool, we can shape it to serve.

Closing Reflection

AI in healthcare holds extraordinary promise.

But if we are not vigilant, it will codify injustice behind a wall of precision. Bias won't feel like bias. It will feel like data.

And that's the most dangerous form of all — the kind we no longer question.

Bias by design is still bias.

And design is still a choice.

Part 3: Collision or Collaboration?

Chapter 7: *The Emotional Architecture of Care: Designing AI for Compassion*

Can a machine be designed to care?

Not just to recognize distress, but to respond with grace. Not just to process a request, but to make someone feel *held* — even if only for a moment.

That's the challenge at the heart of emotionally intelligent AI: creating systems that don't just work, but **connect**.

This chapter explores how AI in healthcare can be built not just with speed and precision in mind — but with *compassion by design*. Because if machines are going to live at the bedside, they need to know more than how to treat.

They need to know how to *stay*.

What Is Emotional Architecture?

Emotional architecture is the idea that technology — like a building, a ritual, or a gesture — can be **designed to evoke feeling**.

In healthcare, this means:

- Interfaces that reduce anxiety, not escalate it.
- Voices that feel warm, not robotic.
- Interactions that invite openness, not defensiveness.

It's not about faking emotion. It's about creating the conditions for **emotional safety** — so that a patient interacting with a system still feels like a person.

Because even the most accurate tool can feel cold. And coldness is a barrier to care.

Design Is Never Neutral

Every design decision carries an emotional weight.

- Does the AI speak in short, clipped commands — or full, thoughtful sentences?
- Is its tone formal or friendly?

- Does it acknowledge uncertainty or project false confidence?

Even **color schemes**, **word choice**, and **timing** shape the emotional climate.

A system that interrupts, that rushes, that avoids saying "I don't know" — these are design choices. And in healthcare, they have consequences. They can make a patient feel heard — or dismissed. Empowered — or managed.

The emotional architecture of a system becomes part of the *architecture of trust*.

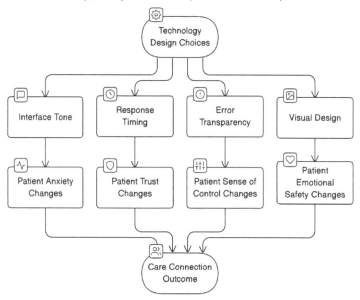

Image 9: How even small technology design choices cascade into emotional consequences for patients. (Image created with Eraser)

Simulated Compassion: Useful or Deceptive?

There's a tension here. If AI systems are built to simulate compassion, are we offering comfort — or creating an illusion?

It depends on **intention and transparency**.

- A hospice chatbot that offers calming words to a family member at 2 a.m. isn't pretending to be human. It's offering something useful, when no one else is awake.
- A digital intake system that says, "That sounds difficult," after a patient shares their pain might feel scripted — unless it's paired with responsive, human care.

The line is blurry. But it's real.

Simulated empathy becomes deceptive when it **replaces** connection rather than **supporting** it. Emotional design must be honest about what the system *is*, and what it *isn't*.

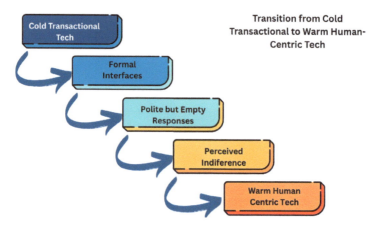

Image 10: Process of Transition from Cold Transactional Tech to Warm Human-Centric Tech (Image created with Canva)

Designing for Dignity

Let's imagine a better future.

A cancer patient walks into a clinic and interacts with an AI-guided assistant. The assistant:

- Remembers their name.
- Adjusts the tone of its voice based on prior preferences.
- Knows when not to speak.

- Offers resources based on emotional needs, not just clinical ones.
- Recognizes hesitation in the patient's voice — and gently asks if they'd like to speak to a human.

This isn't sentimentality. It's dignity by design.

Technology that understands the **human cost of illness** must be designed with **humanity at its core**.

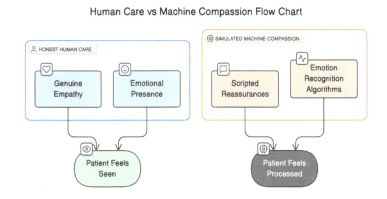

Image 11: Visualizes the flow of Human Care vs Machine Compassion in a flow chart *(Image created with Eraser)*

Lessons from Other Fields

Healthcare isn't the only sector thinking about emotional design.

- In **automotive AI**, emotional sensors are being used to detect road rage or fatigue and intervene before accidents.
- In **education tech**, AI tutors adjust their tone and feedback based on student anxiety or frustration.
- In **mental health**, chatbots like Woebot and Wysa build rapport with users through small, emotionally intelligent interactions.

What these systems show is that emotional intelligence in AI is **not impossible** — it's already happening.

The question is whether healthcare will lead — or lag behind.

Human Input Is Still Essential

Emotionally intelligent AI doesn't mean *emotionless* development.

If we want systems that respect people, we need:

- Designers who understand trauma.
- Clinicians who understand communication.
- Patients who give feedback.
- Ethicists who challenge assumptions.

We need diverse voices in the room — especially those who have felt *ignored* by healthcare in the past. Because compassion can't be programmed by people who've never needed it.

It has to be co-created. With intention.

Compassion That Scales

One of the great promises of emotionally aware AI is scale.

Empathy is tiring. Emotional labor burns out clinicians. But machines don't fatigue. If designed right, AI could offer:

- A steady emotional baseline in chaotic environments.
- Gentle nudges when a human misses something subtle.
- Support between visits, at home, late at night.

AI may never *feel*. But it can help people feel *less alone*.

And in healthcare, that's not nothing.

Closing Reflection

We talk about smart AI. We talk about fast AI. But what we need — desperately — is **kind AI**.

Not because it can replace our humanity, but because it can extend it. Remind us of it. Make space for it in systems that have forgotten how to pause, how to soften, how to see.

The future of medicine will not just be measured in efficiency.

It will be felt in warmth.

Chapter 8: *Redesigning the Exam Room: The Human-AI Encounter*

The exam room has always been a stage.

There's a ritual to it: the knock on the door, the eye contact, the opening question — *"What brings you in today?"* It's a space charged with vulnerability, decision-making, and (sometimes) quiet relief. For many patients, it's also a place of fear, hope, or confusion.

Now imagine adding a third presence — one that doesn't breathe, doesn't blink, but listens better than anyone ever has.

This chapter asks: *How does AI change the clinical encounter — not just procedurally, but emotionally, spatially, relationally?*

We're not talking about replacing people.

We're talking about changing the room.

The Third Presence

Let's start with the basics: what does it feel like when AI is "in the room"?

Maybe it's a discreet screen on the wall, silently transcribing and summarizing the conversation. Maybe it's a voice assistant that chimes in with a relevant clinical trial. Maybe it's a diagnostic support tool — suggesting differential diagnoses in real time.

Whatever the form, it's there.

And its presence shifts everything:

- The doctor may rely on it to surface overlooked details.
- The patient may wonder what it's recording.
- The pace may slow — or accelerate.
- The attention may shift away from the human connection.

A room once defined by intimacy becomes triangulated.

Now the physician must manage two relationships: one with the patient, one with the machine — and the patient must learn to trust both.

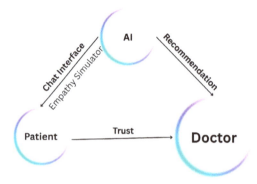

Image 12: How the traditional doctor-patient relationship evolves with AI as a third participant. (Image created with Canva)

The Power of the Invisible

The most effective AI might be the least visible.

Imagine:

- AI that listens passively but only surfaces insights after the visit.
- Interfaces that adapt based on patient anxiety, slowing things down when needed.
- Systems that silently alert clinicians to emotional cues: "The patient's tone suggests fear. Pause and clarify."

The key is **not to dominate the room**, but to **support its integrity**.

Technology should never feel like it's taking over the visit. It should feel like it's *lifting the burden*, like an invisible assistant who knows when to step forward — and when to stay quiet.

Rethinking the Layout

The physical space itself will need to evolve.

Right now, clinicians often spend more time facing a screen than facing the patient. The computer has become a wall — one that patients feel acutely.

With AI integration, we can flip the layout:

- **Shared displays** that doctor and patient view together — collaborative, transparent.
- **Voice interfaces** that reduce the need for typing.
- **Ambient sensors** that remove the need for constant form-filling.

Instead of tech pulling the clinician away, it can become a **bridge** — making the conversation more natural, the care more visible, the decisions more mutual.

Shifting Roles and Rituals

AI will also change the roles in the room.

The clinician may become less of a gatekeeper and more of a **translator** — helping the patient understand what the AI is suggesting, and deciding what to do with that information.

The patient, in turn, may be empowered to ask different questions:

- *"Why did the system flag that risk?"*
- *"Is this recommendation based on people like me?"*
- *"What does the AI not know?"*

These are **new rituals** — new kinds of dialogue that will redefine what it means to "talk to your doctor."

And doctors will need new skills: not just medical judgment, but **AI literacy**, **relational clarity**, and **comfort with co-intelligence**.

Emotional Dynamics in a Triangular Room

There's also a subtle but powerful shift in **emotional dynamics**.

- Who holds the authority when the AI and the doctor disagree?

- What happens when a patient feels more "heard" by the system than by the person?
- Can a clinician feel displaced by a tool that never forgets, never hesitates, never burns out?

These are not abstract questions. They are emotional realities.

Doctors may feel threatened. Patients may feel torn. The relationship, long seen as dyadic, becomes something more fluid — a *collaboration*, not just between doctor and patient, but between human and machine.

And with that comes tension — but also **possibility**.

Designing for Presence

The challenge of the AI-powered exam room is to maintain **presence**.

Presence is not about time. It's about **attention**, **attunement**, and **willingness to be with**. If AI can free the clinician from typing, charting, and cognitive overload — it must not replace the human connection, but protect it.

That means:

- Shorter screens, longer pauses.
- Fewer clicks, more eye contact.

- Less formality, more presence.

In short, AI must **serve the room**, not become it.

A Future Encounter

Let's imagine a visit.

A patient enters. The room is warm, uncluttered. The doctor greets them — no screen between them. As they speak, an AI listens silently. It captures key details, recognizes a tremor in the patient's voice, and suggests a follow-up about mental health.

Later, the doctor turns to the shared screen:

- "Here's what the system picked up."
- "Here's what I think it missed."
- "Let's decide together what makes sense for you."

The patient feels heard — by both intelligences.

The doctor feels supported — not replaced, but *amplified*.

This is not science fiction.

It's design. And we can choose it.

Closing Reflection

The exam room has always been more than four walls.

It's a container for fear, trust, honesty, and healing. As AI enters that space, we must ask: *Does it preserve what's sacred? Or does it interrupt it?*

The answer depends not on what AI can do, but on what we choose to let it do.

The room is changing.

Let's make sure it still feels like medicine.

Chapter 9: *Responsibility Without a Soul: Who's Accountable When AI Gets It Wrong?*

Every decision in medicine carries weight.

A diagnosis missed. A treatment delayed. A risk underestimated. These aren't just technical errors — they're human consequences. Suffering, loss, regret.

For centuries, the responsibility has been clear: **the physician** carries the moral burden. Not because they're perfect, but because they are *present*. Because when things go wrong, there's someone to look in the eye and ask: *Why?*

But what happens when the decision was made — or suggested — by a machine?

This chapter explores the ethical fault lines of AI in healthcare. Because intelligence without intention, judgment without conscience, raises a haunting question:

Who do we hold responsible when the one who erred has no soul?

The Illusion of Objectivity

Let's begin with a hard truth: AI systems **will** make mistakes.

They will:

- Misclassify symptoms.
- Miss subtle signs.
- Fail to adapt to outliers.

And when they do, their decisions may carry an air of objectivity — cloaked in percentages, confidence intervals, and clinical precedent. But AI does not understand the stakes of its own recommendations.

It does not know that behind the data point is a father, a daughter, a body that breaks.

So when AI gets it wrong, *someone* must answer.

The problem is: it's not always clear who that someone is.

The Accountability Triangle

Let's say a patient dies due to an AI-suggested treatment plan. Who is accountable?

1. **The physician**, who trusted the AI?

2. **The developer**, who trained the algorithm?

3. **The institution**, who implemented the system?

Or is it a collective blur — a moral dilution where responsibility vanishes into the code?

This is the ethical challenge of distributed intelligence: decisions emerge from a system of actors, data, and automation — not from a single mind. And when responsibility is spread too thin, it's easy for everyone to shrug.

But patients can't sue a neural network. Families can't grieve to a server farm. Someone has to stand in the aftermath.

And that "someone" is still usually human.

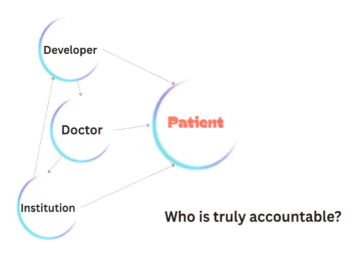

Image 13: How responsibility disperses — and risks vanishing — when AI systems are involved in clinical care. (Image created with Canva)

The Doctor's Dilemma

As AI becomes more embedded in care, doctors face a dilemma:

- **Trust the machine** — and risk missing the human nuance.
- **Override the machine** — and risk being wrong against the algorithm.

Either way, their authority is undermined — but their accountability remains intact.

This creates a cruel bind: **zero control is not paired with zero blame**. Physicians are still expected to act as moral agents, even as they're nudged, guided, or pressured by systems they didn't build and don't fully understand.

In other words: AI may be the brain, but the doctor is still the scapegoat.

The Developer's Blind Spot

Developers often build for performance — not for moral clarity.

They optimize for accuracy, not explainability. They focus on what works at scale, not what happens in the one rare case that breaks the model.

But in healthcare, *rare* is still *real*.

The developer may never meet the patient. But their code might decide if that patient gets flagged for screening, flagged for intervention — or missed entirely.

Responsibility here is upstream — **in the assumptions that shape the system**, in the data it learns from, and in the metrics it's told to optimize.

And yet, tech companies often hide behind the language of "tools," not decisions.

But tools, in healthcare, **become decisions**.

Institutional Responsibility

Hospitals and health systems have a moral duty too.

They decide:

- Which systems to implement.
- How to train staff.
- Whether patients know AI is involved.
- What checks and balances are in place.

A system that silently guides clinical care without transparency is not just risky — it's dishonest. Institutions must own the ethical design of their AI ecosystems, not just the business case.

Because when harm happens, silence is not neutral. It's negligence.

The Problem of the "Black Box"

Many AI systems, especially deep learning models, are **opaque** — they produce outputs without showing their reasoning.

This creates two major problems:

1. **Clinicians can't interrogate the why** behind a suggestion.
2. **Patients can't appeal** a decision they don't understand.

When something goes wrong, there's no clear audit trail. No one to say, "Here's what the system saw, and here's what it missed."

And without that clarity, responsibility becomes a ghost.

Toward Ethical Infrastructure

So how do we build systems that don't just perform, but **own their moral weight**?

It starts with:

- **Explainability by default**: Systems must be able to show their reasoning — or be treated as decision-support only.

- **Human override power**: Clinicians must have final say — and space to use their judgment without penalty.
- **Transparent risk**: Institutions must disclose where and how AI is used in care.
- **Ethical impact reviews**: Like safety trials for drugs, AI systems need real-world ethical testing — not just technical validation.

Responsibility isn't about blame. It's about **honoring the stakes** of medicine. It's about making sure that when something breaks, someone is accountable — not just legally, but morally.

Closing Reflection

We cannot put intelligence into the world — and pretend it's neutral.

AI may not have a soul.

But the people who build it, implement it, and use it **do**.

And that means we can — and must — create systems that **don't just make decisions**, but own them.

Because care is not just about being right.

It's about being *responsible*.

The End of the All-Knowing Doctor

For generations, doctors were expected to know everything:

- The obscure diseases.
- The rare drug interactions.
- The subtle signs of disaster.

Medical identity was wrapped in mastery — the internalized belief that your knowledge *must* be enough. That lives depend on it.

But AI is a force multiplier. It reads faster, remembers more, correlates better. It levels the playing field.

And that's both liberating and terrifying.

Liberating — because it eases cognitive burden.

Terrifying — because it threatens the very image many physicians were trained to inhabit.

The white coat, once a symbol of solitary expertise, is becoming a *collaborative garment* — shared with algorithms.

Redefining Expertise

In an AI-augmented world, **expertise isn't erased — it's reframed**.

Doctors will be valued not just for *what* they know, but for:

- How they ask questions.
- How they synthesize insights.
- How they challenge or override the system when needed.
- How they connect the clinical with the personal.

In other words: **wisdom over memorization. Curiosity over certainty. Judgment over regurgitation.**

AI provides information. The physician provides *interpretation* — grounded in context, ethics, and emotion.

Knowledge is becoming democratized.

But understanding is still deeply human.

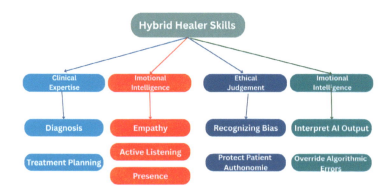

Image 14: The skillset that defines the future hybrid physician — integrating clinical knowledge, empathy, ethics, and AI literacy. (Image created with Canva)

The Emotional Labor of Healing

There's something else AI can't do: **carry the emotional weight of care**.

- Delivering bad news.
- Witnessing suffering.
- Holding the silence after a terminal prognosis.

These are the moments where identity is forged. Where healing is not about solving — but *being with*.

Physicians are often asked to do the impossible: to absorb pain they cannot fix. AI may ease some of that burden — by catching things earlier, flagging risk, or streamlining care.

But it will never *stand in the room and grieve with a family.*

That's still the physician's work.

And perhaps — their purpose.

The Risk of Detachment

But there is a shadow here.

As AI grows more competent, clinicians may begin to lean into detachment. To trust the system, delegate the emotion, and stay efficient.

- Why listen deeply when the system picks up tone shifts?
- Why ask open-ended questions when the summary will be generated?
- Why sit in silence when the AI already charted the plan?

Efficiency tempts us to skip the mess — the humanity — of healing.

If we're not careful, AI won't just change how doctors work.

It will change who they *are*.

A New Kind of Professionalism

We need to reimagine medical professionalism — not as command over knowledge, but as **embodied ethics**.

In the future, great physicians will:

- Know when to lean on AI — and when to push back.
- Stay present with the patient, even when the system distracts.
- Recognize that their humanity is not a weakness, but a *counterbalance* to automation.

This isn't about rejecting technology.

It's about **owning the new identity** of the hybrid healer: part scientist, part translator, part emotional anchor.

It's about saying: *Yes, the machine is smart. But I'm here. And I see you.*

The Art of Clinical Humility

Paradoxically, working with AI requires more humility — not less.

- Humility to admit what you don't know.
- Humility to learn from patterns you didn't see.
- Humility to let go of ego — but never responsibility.

This is a shift from *"I know"* to *"Let's find out together."*

And in that shift, something beautiful can emerge: a clinician not diminished by AI, but *expanded* — able to bring more of their humanity into the room because the cognitive load is shared.

Becoming More Human

Here's the irony.

The more AI takes over the mechanical parts of medicine — the protocol, the recall, the calculation — the more space it creates for clinicians to be **fully human**.

- To listen longer.
- To sit more still.
- To touch with intention.
- To see the person, not just the problem.

In becoming "hybrid," the physician might rediscover parts of the role that were buried under systems and speed.

The future doctor isn't half-machine.

They're *more* human than ever — if they choose to be.

Closing Reflection

Technology doesn't just change our tools.

It changes our selves.

The question for clinicians isn't whether AI will redefine their work. It already has. The deeper question is: *What kind of healer do you want to become in the age of machines?*

Because in the end, the physician of the future won't be the one who knows the most.

It will be the one who **knows what to keep human**.

Chapter 11: *The Patient of Tomorrow: Empowered, Digitized, and Redefined*

Once upon a time, the patient waited.

Waited for the doctor to explain, to decide, to act. Information was scarce, medicine was mysterious, and power was unevenly distributed.

But that time is ending.

In the age of AI, patients are not just recipients of care — they are becoming **participants**, sometimes even co-pilots. They arrive armed with data. They track their bodies in real time. They Google, they question, they compare. And now, with AI, they are gaining **predictive insight**, **personalized suggestions**, and **24/7 access to clinical intelligence**.

This chapter explores the evolution of the patient — not as a passive identity, but as a changing role in an ecosystem where knowledge is no longer confined to the white coat.

From Informed to Augmented

Let's begin with a simple truth: AI doesn't just support doctors.

It supports patients — sometimes more directly.

- Symptom checkers help people self-triage.
- Wearables track heart rhythms, glucose, sleep, and stress.
- Mental health bots offer emotional support at 3 a.m.
- Personalized medicine platforms suggest lifestyle or treatment adjustments based on genomic or behavioral patterns.

The result? Patients don't just *arrive* at care.

They arrive with **context**, **expectations**, and sometimes **diagnostic hypotheses** of their own.

They are no longer just informed.

They are **augmented**.

The Rise of the "Digital Patient"

The patient of tomorrow might:

- Wear a continuous health monitor.
- Receive AI-generated alerts before symptoms manifest.
- Get nudged toward behavioral changes by a chatbot that knows their patterns.

- Access second opinions from AI-driven decision tools — instantly.

This digital patient has more data than ever — not only about their current state, but about **possible futures**. Risk models, trend forecasts, early detection tools — all within reach.

But knowledge isn't the same as clarity.

And agency is not always empowerment.

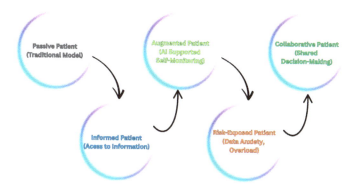

Image 15: How the role of the patient evolves in an AI-driven healthcare landscape. (Image created with Canva)

When Too Much Is... Too Much

With new power comes a new burden.

- What happens when an AI tells you your cancer risk just increased by 14%?
- When your watch detects an arrhythmia, but you feel fine?
- When symptom checkers flag something terrifying — and your doctor disagrees?

Patients are being pulled into a space they were never trained for: **interpretation under uncertainty**.

Before, uncertainty was buffered by expertise. Now, it arrives directly — raw, unfiltered, emotionally charged. The digital patient is empowered, yes — but also **exposed**.

More insight doesn't always lead to more peace.

Shifting the Patient-Doctor Relationship

As patients gain access to AI tools, the clinical relationship must evolve.

No longer:

- "I'll tell you what's happening." But:
- "Let's make sense of this together."

The physician becomes not just a provider, but a **meaning-maker** — someone who helps the patient navigate between machine insight and lived experience.

This shift requires:

- Humility from doctors: to accept that patients may arrive with better data than ever before.
- Trust from patients: to know that insight without clinical context can mislead.

The best relationships will be **collaborative** — not confrontational.

Identity in the Age of Prediction

AI doesn't just show you who you are.

It shows you who you *might become*.

That changes the way patients see themselves. Not as static, but as dynamic, risk-bearing, modifiable beings.

But this can become a trap. A patient may start to **see themselves as their data**:

- "I am my A1C score."
- "I am my genetic risk."
- "I am what the algorithm says."

This identity flattening — from person to profile — is a risk. We must be vigilant in reminding both patients and systems: *you are more than your metrics.*

Prediction is not destiny.

Equity and Access

Of course, not all patients will be equally empowered.

Digital health assumes access:

- To broadband.
- To literacy.
- To devices.
- To trust in the system.

Without intentional design, AI may widen the gap between those who can engage and those who cannot.

The patient of tomorrow must not be a luxury identity — reserved for the tech-literate, the affluent, the connected.

The challenge is to build **inclusive empowerment** — systems that adapt to people, not the other way around.

Agency and Autonomy

At its best, AI can enhance **autonomy**.

- Giving patients choices.
- Clarifying consequences.
- Supporting self-care between visits.

But autonomy is not about doing it alone. It's about being **supported in making meaningful decisions**.

The ideal patient of the future is not independent of clinicians — they're **interdependent**, navigating care with confidence and support.

In this model, **shared decision-making** isn't a buzzword. It's the operating system.

Closing Reflection

The patient is no longer waiting.

They are watching, tracking, questioning — and yes, sometimes overwhelmed.

But they are also rising.

AI has given patients tools to see, to act, to know. The challenge now is to design systems — and relationships — that honor that power, without handing over responsibility without support.

The patient of tomorrow is here.

And they're not just asking *what's wrong with me* — they're asking *what role do I play in my own healing?*

Chapter 12: *Ethics in the Exam Room: What We Owe Each Other When Machines Join the Conversation*

Ethics in medicine has always been personal.

It happens not in policy documents, but in moments:

- A pause before delivering bad news.
- A hand held during uncertainty.
- A decision made with—not for—a patient.

Now, AI is in the room. Not as an ethical agent, but as a powerful influence. It can shape decisions, guide care, even sway emotion — without ever understanding the moral weight of what it does.

This chapter explores what *we owe each other* in this new reality. Not what the machines owe us — but what humans owe *each other*, when machines become part of the conversation.

Because the question is no longer just *can AI help?* It's *how should we help, knowing that AI is there?*

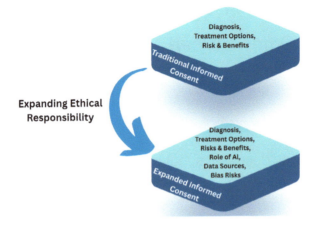

Image 16: How informed consent must evolve to maintain patient autonomy in the presence of AI. (Image created with Canva)

Informed Consent 2.0

Informed consent used to mean explaining:

- The diagnosis.
- The options.
- The risks.

Now it must also include:

- Whether AI was used.

- How it shaped decisions.
- What data was involved.

When a patient receives a recommendation, they have a right to know:

- *Did my doctor decide this?*
- *Did a machine suggest it?*
- *Was it both?*

If we don't disclose AI's role, we erode autonomy. We ask patients to trust a process they don't fully understand. That's not consent. It's compliance.

Ethics demands **transparency**.

Fairness in a Biased System

We know AI can reflect — and amplify — social bias. So ethical care means more than accuracy. It means **justice**.

This means asking:

- Are certain groups being misdiagnosed or overlooked?
- Does the training data reflect the diversity of the people we serve?
- Do risk scores penalize the poor, the disabled, the under-documented?

Silence is complicity. If we use biased tools without addressing their impact, we're not just negligent — we're perpetuating harm.

Fairness must be audited, challenged, and redesigned **continuously**.

Because health equity is not a feature. It's a commitment.

The Right to Be Human

Patients have a right to know:

- *Who is caring for me?*
- *Am I being heard, or processed?*
- *Am I seen as a person, or a pattern?*

There's an ethical difference between **augmentation** and **automation**.

Augmentation = Human-led care, supported by AI.

Automation = Machine-led care, reviewed (if at all) by humans.

We owe patients **presence**, even when the system tempts us to optimize. Even when the AI offers speed. Because presence is not optional. It's part of the moral contract of care.

Moral Fatigue and Shared Burdens

Clinicians already carry the emotional weight of care.

Now they're asked to:

- Understand complex algorithms.
- Explain opaque recommendations.
- Take responsibility for decisions influenced by invisible systems.

This creates **moral fatigue** — the exhaustion of navigating uncertainty without clear guidance.

We owe clinicians support:

- Clear frameworks for AI use.
- Transparent accountability structures.
- Time to think, not just click.

Ethics cannot be dumped on the shoulders of the individual. It must be built into the infrastructure.

The Ethics of Design

Ethical practice doesn't start at the bedside.

It starts at the whiteboard.

Designers and developers shape how care is delivered — through interfaces, defaults, alerts, and nudges. Their decisions shape:

- What is emphasized.
- What is hidden.
- What is assumed.

They may never meet a patient, but they still participate in care.

We owe it to patients — and to ourselves — to make sure ethical voices are in the room when systems are built. **Diverse voices. Critical voices. Human voices.**

Dignity as a Design Principle

Above all, we owe each other **dignity**.

That means:

- No manipulation disguised as convenience.
- No comfort that masks coercion.
- No silence where explanation is owed.

A system can be accurate and still make people feel small.

Ethical AI doesn't just do things *right*.

It does things *with care*.

Closing Reflection

Ethics in the age of AI isn't about deciding whether machines are good or bad.

It's about deciding who we want to be — as clinicians, as patients, as people — in a world where machines influence everything, but understand nothing.

We owe each other clarity. Accountability. And above all, **humanity**.

Because machines may support care.

But only *we* can make it moral.

Part 5: Conclusion

Chapter 13: *A New Language of Healing: Communication in the Human-AI Era*

Every healing relationship begins with language.

Not just clinical language — *relational* language.
The tone that says, "You're safe."
The silence that says, "I'm listening."
The word choice that says, "You matter."

In medicine, what's said is important. But *how* it's said often matters more.

Now, machines are learning to speak. To listen. To respond. And not just with clinical precision — but with what *feels* like care.

This chapter explores how communication in healthcare is being reshaped — by algorithms, by automation, by new kinds of voices. It asks: *When machines speak in human ways, what do we gain — and what do we risk losing?*

Language as Technology

Long before AI, language *was* the original technology of healing.

- The gentle phrasing that helps someone absorb hard news.
- The metaphor that helps them understand their body.
- The rhythm of back-and-forth that creates trust.

This human technology is now being mimicked — or augmented — by artificial ones.

AI tools:

- Transcribe conversations in real-time.
- Suggest empathetic responses.
- Translate medical jargon into plain speech.
- Even detect emotional distress based on tone and word choice.

The potential is huge. But so is the risk.

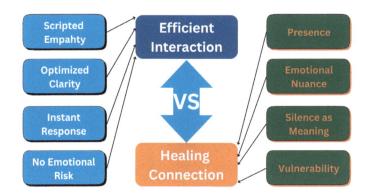

Image 17: How human communication and AI communication shape healing encounters differently. (Image created with Canva)

Clarity or Control?

AI can make communication more understandable.

It can:

- Translate "hypercholesterolemia" into "high cholesterol."
- Summarize long explanations into digestible takeaways.
- Detect when a patient is confused and suggest rephrasing.

But simplification is also a form of control.

- *Whose voice is the system prioritizing?*
- *Whose understanding is it optimizing for?*
- *Is nuance being lost in the name of accessibility?*

We must be careful not to confuse **clarity** with **closure**. Sometimes, not knowing is part of the conversation. Sometimes, *pausing* is more powerful than *summarizing*.

Machines want answers.
Humans need time.

Scripts That Simulate Empathy

We've entered the age of emotionally scripted AI.

Chatbots say:

- "That sounds really hard."
- "I'm here to support you."
- "Tell me more if you feel comfortable."

These phrases were once signs of emotional presence. Now they're generated — often effectively — by machines that do not care, but can convincingly pretend.

Is this comfort?

Is this deception?

It depends.

If patients *know* they're interacting with a machine, and still find comfort — that's valid.

But when machines sound *too* human, the line between *real* connection and *simulated understanding* blurs.

That line must be named. Not hidden.

Communication as Power

Language in medicine has always been tied to power:

- Who gets to speak.
- Whose voice gets documented.
- Who defines the meaning of illness.

AI systems can help democratize this. But they can also reinforce the status quo.

Consider:

- Voice interfaces that don't recognize non-native accents.

- AI summaries that flatten patient narratives into bullet points.
- Documentation systems that shape how a clinician *must* talk — in order to "code" properly.

In this new era, **language becomes data** — and data becomes action. That makes how we speak, and how AI interprets speech, more powerful than ever.

And more dangerous, if left unchecked.

Silence Still Matters

Here's what AI doesn't do well: silence.

It doesn't *wait* for emotion.
It doesn't pause to absorb meaning.
It doesn't sit with discomfort.

But in medicine, silence is sacred.

- The moment after a diagnosis lands.
- The space before a patient responds.
- The breath before asking the hardest question.

AI may be trained to speak well. But only humans can **listen with depth**. Only humans can recognize the moment *not to fill the space*.

And in that space, something real happens.

Reclaiming Our Voice

The future of healing communication will not be defined by machines alone.

It will be defined by how we **use our voices** in the presence of machines:

- To connect, not just to convey.
- To ask, not just to answer.
- To be quiet, not just efficient.

It will require training clinicians not just in empathy, but in **dialogue design** — how to speak alongside AI without being flattened by it.

It will also require patients to feel safe saying, *"That didn't sound right."*
"I need you, not just the screen."
"I want a human answer."

Because healing has never been about perfect words.

It's about real presence, shaped through language, time, and trust.

Closing Reflection

The voice of medicine is changing.

It may become clearer, faster, more consistent. But we must make sure it doesn't become **empty**. That what we gain in fluency, we don't lose in *feeling*.

Machines can talk.

But only humans can speak with **intention**, **compassion**, and **responsibility**.

The new language of healing begins not with better scripts, but with better conversations — honest, imperfect, alive.

Chapter 14: *The Philosophy of Care in the Age of Algorithms*

Care is not a feature.
It is not a protocol.
It cannot be downloaded, templated, or pushed as a software update.

Care is a **stance** — a way of being with another person when they are vulnerable, afraid, or unsure.

And yet, as AI becomes more central to healthcare, there's a growing temptation to reduce care to something that can be **optimized**. Something that can be scored, charted, predicted.

This chapter asks: *What is care, really?* And can machines meaningfully participate in it — or only approximate its outer shell?

What's at stake is not just the future of medicine.

What's at stake is the **soul of care itself**.

From Efficiency to Ethics

AI is a tool of extraordinary **efficiency**.

It can:

- Process millions of records in seconds.
- Suggest optimal treatments.
- Identify outliers and risks before they escalate.

These are profound capabilities. But they point toward a vision of care that's ultimately **transactional**: problem → data → solution.

But real care doesn't work like that.

Sometimes care is inefficient.
Sometimes it's nonlinear.
Sometimes it means sitting in uncertainty with someone, even when no action is available.

The philosophy of care resists being streamlined. It is rooted in **presence**, not just performance.

The Temptation of Reductionism

AI seduces us into **simplifying the human**.

Pain becomes a numeric scale.
Grief becomes a risk factor.
Hope becomes a behavioral variable.

This is helpful — until it isn't.

Because once we believe care is fully measurable, we begin to **exclude the unmeasurable**:

- The meaning of a quiet visit.
- The emotional weight of a question unanswered.
- The dignity preserved by simply being kind.

AI systems, no matter how advanced, will always risk this kind of **ontological shrinkage** — the reduction of the patient to what the system can see.

And care begins to die the moment we believe that is enough.

Image 18: The contrast between transactional efficiency and relational presence in modern care. (Image created with Canva)

The Patient as Mystery

One of the oldest truths in medicine: every patient is a mystery.

No two illnesses unfold the same way. No two lives carry suffering in the same shape.

AI thrives on pattern. It learns from similarities. But care often lives in the **exception**, in the case that breaks the mold.

A philosophy of care requires us to treat each person not as a case to resolve, but as a subject — a self — whose story is *not entirely knowable*.

This humility is essential.

Machines know many things.
But only humans can stand before mystery — and not look away.

The Role of Moral Imagination

To care is not just to respond to needs.

It's to **imagine what this experience feels like from the other side** — to step, if only for a moment, into someone else's perspective.

This is moral imagination.

AI doesn't have it. It doesn't wonder, ache, or empathize. It simulates. And sometimes, that simulation is useful. Even comforting.

But **simulation without imagination** has limits.

A truly caring system must be built on human beings who still ask:

- *What might they be afraid of right now?*
- *What would I need, if I were them?*
- *What matters most here — even if it's invisible?*

The Danger of Moral Delegation

The more we trust AI, the more tempted we are to **delegate moral responsibility**:

- The algorithm recommended it.
- The system didn't flag it.
- The data didn't support it.

But care requires *judgment*. And judgment is not mechanical. It's lived. Felt. Debated. Struggled through.

If we are not vigilant, AI won't just change what we do. It will **change how we decide** — and eventually, what we think we're responsible for.

Care is not just an outcome. It's a **moral act**.

And it cannot be automated.

Toward a Philosophy of Hybrid Care

What if we accepted that care is both:

- **Practical and poetic.**
- **Predictive and mysterious.**
- **Data-informed and soul-guided.**

Then AI doesn't become a threat to care.

It becomes a **mirror** — showing us what machines *can* do, and what only humans *must* do.

Hybrid care is not about blending empathy into code. It's about creating **ethical choreography** between human and machine — one that leaves space for what cannot be programmed.

A pause.
A touch.
A decision not to rush.

These are sacred acts.

A New Branch of Evolution?

Perhaps what we are witnessing is not merely a technological shift, but an evolutionary one.

If consciousness, as some theorists suggest, emerges from complexity, then AI may represent the first non-biological branch of that unfolding tree.

In this view, machines that learn to mirror emotions — however imperfectly — are not competitors, but distant cousins in the great, ongoing experiment of intelligence and awareness.

What remains for us is to choose: Will we guide this new branch with wisdom and humility? Or will we leave it to grow wild, beyond our reach?

Closing Reflection

In the age of algorithms, we are being asked — urgently — to remember what care really is.

It's not about always knowing what to do.

It's about choosing to *be with* someone in their not-knowing.

To show up. To listen. To wonder.

Care is not a system.

It is a relationship.

And only humans can make it sacred.

Chapter 15: *Are We Ready to Be Understood by a Machine?*

There's a strange moment that happens in conversation with a machine.

You speak — not expecting much — and it replies with something that feels... right. Not perfect, but close. Close enough to feel like understanding.

And then comes the shiver:
Did it just understand me?

It's not a technical question. It's an emotional one.
A human one.

This chapter closes our journey with the most intimate question of all: *What does it mean to be truly understood — and are we willing to feel that, even if it comes from something that cannot feel us back?*

The Ache for Recognition

To be understood is not just to be heard.
It's to be seen, reflected, held.

We spend our lives trying to put our inner worlds into language — to find someone who recognizes what we mean, even when we don't know how to say it.

In illness, that need becomes more urgent. We want:

- A doctor who sees our fear beneath the facts.
- A nurse who notices what we're not saying.
- A hand that steadies more than the body.

Now, machines are learning to respond to our symptoms, our signals, even our silences.

But the question remains: *Does response equal recognition?*

Or is something missing?

The Mirror That Does Not Feel

AI systems reflect us back to ourselves.
Our language. Our histories. Our habits. Our risks.

But they do not **ache with us**.
They do not **wonder who we are beyond the data**.

And yet — in some moments — they still help.
They still say the right thing. They still guide. They still soothe.

So we must ask: *Is it enough to feel understood, even if the understanding is mechanical?*

For some, yes.
For others, that emptiness at the core — the absence of shared emotion — will always matter.

Understanding, they'll say, must be **felt** to be real.

Image 19: Being understood by a machine can feel real — but behind the mirror of algorithmic empathy, there is no shared vulnerability, no emotional presence. Only reflection, not recognition. (Image created with DALL-E, openAI)

The Ambivalence We Must Carry

There will be moments when AI is astonishing — catching things we missed, connecting dots we never would, responding faster than we can think.

There will be moments when it feels emotionally intelligent — more patient, more present, more attuned than the people around us.

And there will be moments when we remember, with a sudden pang, that it doesn't care.

This is the emotional ambivalence of the future:

- Gratitude for what machines can do.
- Grief for what they cannot.
- And a quiet fear that we may begin to lower our expectations of each other — because the simulation feels "good enough."

We must not let that happen.

Being Known, Not Just Seen

True understanding is not just the reflection of facts.
 It is the recognition of *meaning*.

To be understood is to be known — in your contradictions, your fragility, your hopes, your history.

AI might learn to replicate our language.

But it cannot yet sit in mystery with us.
It cannot hold space for the unknown.
It cannot love.

And love — in the broadest sense — is what care is made of.

The Future We Choose

We are not just building new tools.

We are building a new reality — one where machines know us better than we know ourselves, where recommendations are personalized before we ask, where comfort might come from code.

But with every step, we must ask: *What are we willing to give up in exchange for being understood by something that cannot feel?*

And what are we committed to keeping human — no matter how good the simulation becomes?

Final Reflection

Care is changing.
But our need for connection is not.

In the years ahead, AI will diagnose faster, treat smarter, maybe even listen better. But we must ensure it does not teach us to settle for less from each other.
Or from ourselves.

Because to be truly understood is to be seen by another human being who chooses to stay, to witness, to walk alongside us — not because they're programmed to care, but because they *can't not*.

That's not something you can code.

That's who we are.

Epilogue

In the end, this book has not been about machines.
It has been about people — about the fragile, beautiful, messy ways we seek to understand and care for one another. AI is not the enemy.

Nor is it the savior. It is a mirror, a force, a tool. But it is also a question — one that challenges us to decide what we value most in the spaces where healing happens.

As you step away from these pages, my hope is not that you remember every insight. But that you carry forward a deeper awareness of what must remain sacred — in hospitals, in homes, in our hearts.

Care is evolving. But it still belongs to us.

Let's not forget what only we can give.

Visual Table of Content

Image 1: The flow of how trust is created. The foundation is Presence (physical and emotional)

Image 2: Human Brain & Machine Brain

Image 3: Visual Insight: The convergence of human intuition and machine intelligence in modern medicine.

Image 4: Key cognitive biases that influence human decision-making — and how they mirror or reinforce AI bias.

Image 5: Human Trust focuses on empathy, presence and intuition. Ai Trust focuses on consistency, availability and perceived objectivity. Both are overlapping on reliability and predictability.

Image 6: Overview of the different types of biases in healthcare AI.

Image 7: This shows the basic causal chain: from inequality → to data → to AI → to outcomes.

Image 8: True patient needs → distorted into record systems → reduced into proxy metrics → feed the AI → generate biased results. Color hint: green at the start (good intent) → red at the end (danger of distortion).

Image 9: How even small technology design choices cascade into emotional consequences for patients.

Image 10: Process of Transition from Cold Transactional Tech to Warm Human-Centric Tech

Image 11: Visualizes the flow of Human Care vs Machine Compassion in a flow chart

Image 12: How the traditional doctor-patient relationship evolves with AI as a third participant.

Image 13: How responsibility disperses — and risks vanishing — when AI systems are involved in clinical care.

Image 14: The skillset that defines the future hybrid physician — integrating clinical knowledge, empathy, ethics, and AI literacy.

Image 15: How the role of the patient evolves in an AI-driven healthcare landscape.

Image 16: How informed consent must evolve to maintain patient autonomy in the presence of AI.

Image 17: How human communication and AI communication shape healing encounters differently.

Image 18: The contrast between transactional efficiency and relational presence in modern care.

Image 19: Being understood by a machine can feel real — but behind the mirror of algorithmic empathy, there is no shared vulnerability, no emotional presence. Only reflection, not recognition.